THE JOURNEY
OF STABAT

Roschelle Ridenhour

Printed in the United States of America
First Edition: April 2017
Edited by Stuart Englert
Cover template by CreateSpace
Cover photo © Shutterstock/Protasov AN

Library of Congress Cataloging-in-Publication
Data

Roschelle Ridenhour
The Journey of Stabat/Roschelle Ridenhour

Summary: "A vengeful woman grieving over
the loss of her husband and son discovers
forgiveness and healing on her journey to find
justice."

ISBN: 978-0-979-0696-1-1 (paperback) :
1.Stabat Mater—United States 2. Journey—
United States 3. Grief—United States. 4.
Justice—United States. 5. Healing—United
States. 6. Forgiveness—United States 7. Jesus—
United States

"Dear God,

I am so afraid to open my clenched fists! Who will I be when I have nothing left to hold on to? Who will I be when I stand before you with empty hands? Please help me to gradually open my hands and discover that I am not what I own, but what you want to give me."

—Henri J.M. Nouven

The Only Necessary Thing: Living a Prayerful Life

~ • ~

The thief had stolen so much from her. He had taken all that was dear and precious in her life. The last morsel of hope that Stabat clung to was that she would be able to watch him die, to finally watch him get what he deserved. The time had come. The time she had waited for. Once he was gone, she would be at rest. The pain and the loss would subside. "Oh, how he deserved to die," Stabat thought.

Stabat awoke before sunrise, and having no oil to light the lamp, she lay in darkness, absorbing the stillness. After a restless night, and weak from not eating for several days, staying in bed provided a small comfort to the grieving widow and mother. As much as she had longed for revenge, now that the time had arrived, the three-day journey ahead seemed foreboding. She needed her strength, she had to make the trip, and she knew she had to follow through to see justice served. These were her thoughts as she closed her eyes and slowly drifted back to sleep. All too soon, sunlight crept through the cracks and crevices of her mud and stick home, as if it were an illuminating voice saying, "Rise! It is time. It is time."

Her humble farm home didn't hold much. Three stools surrounded a round wooden table. In one corner was a sheep skin-covered bed; in the other, a simple wooden bench. Draped across the bench was a thin, threadbare scarf. Beside the bench stood a chest, packed with all of Stabat's clothing and earthly possessions. The shelves were almost bare, other than a few cups and bowls, and some urns containing spices.

As Stabat sat at the table, her thoughts running amuck, she tried not to be consumed with the past. However, her recollections weighed on her as heavy as prison chains. She finished the last bit of wine in her cracked mug and turned her attention to packing what little food she had. After putting a leftover piece of dried fish, two large figs and a jug of water in a small bucket, she covered the container with a piece of cloth and tied it with a string. If she met someone on the road, she wanted them to think that all of the food she had was in the bucket.

She divided a small loaf of bread on the table in half and ate the smaller portion with the remaining dab of honey. The few crumbs that landed on the table were swooshed up by her tiny, frail hands then cupped to her lips. She wrapped the remaining bread tightly in her only scarf and held it close to her cheek. The scarf had been a gift from her husband. Wear and washing had faded its once bright red, green and black pattern. The ends were frayed and the material so threadbare that she feared it would fall apart before her journey's end. Next, she placed two small coins in a scrap of cloth and tucked the makeshift purse next to the bread. She tied the scarf around her waist and twisted it to the side.

She thought it best to hide the bread and money for fear of being robbed along the road. The land was barren from the drought and people were desperate. It was dangerous enough for a woman to be walking alone and she didn't want to appear as if she had anything worth stealing. For a moment her heart sank and, if she had allowed it, her grief would have brought her to tears. Instead, she experienced a melancholy moment.

Though sparse, her home held plenty of wonderful memories. She remembers a time when the garden was bountiful, and her home full of love and laughter. As an orchard worker, her husband had been a skilled gardener. He was smart and he knew when to plant the seeds that he saved from year to year. Their son, barely old enough to walk, followed him around the garden. Whatever Samuel did, their son, little Samuel, did as well. How many times had she and her husband worked until sundown, tending the crops? Though the work was difficult, the sweat and toil was of little consequence for all of the wonderful fruits and vegetables they harvested and enjoyed. How many times had she picked peas and sliced melon while envisioning how her son would grow up and become a good man like his father?

But today Stabat didn't have time to dwell in the past. She chided herself for her foolish reminiscing, which only brought despair. She had a journey ahead, and she had to prepare to leave.

Although warm in the day, she knew it would be cool at night. Though she didn't have many clothes to choose from, she only wanted to take what was needed. She considered wearing two dresses but then determined that would be too cumbersome. She also considered wearing two tunics, but decided one and her shawl would be adequate. She was about to put the second tunic back in the chest when her hands slid down the wooden box, quivering as they lay on the leather handle. She knelt in contemplation for a few minutes before opening the chest crafted by her husband. On top lay the bundle of swaddling clothes that little Samuel was wrapped in on the night of his birth. Along with the infant wraps were the toddler's two tiny tunics. Stabat realized that if he had lived, he soon would have outgrown the garments. She remembers secretly thinking that she might use the tunic fabric to make a doll for the daughter she yearned to have with her husband. A gourd baby rattle and a small leather ball also lay in the chest. She buried her face in the swaddling clothes, trying to absorb the memories, trying to hold on to all that she had lost. Yet, all that was left were a few keepsakes of little Samuel's short life. She closed the chest on the only proof that her child once had lived.

With a tear in her eye, Stabat stood up and grabbed her woolen shawl. Over time, its dark green color had faded to a lighter hue. As she drew the wrap around her shoulders, she thought about the last time she held little Samuel, how she had bundled him in the warm shawl hoping it would keep the feverish boy from shaking. It did not.

Emotions overtook her again as she looked around the home where she had lived since she married Samuel 12 years ago. For a fleeting moment, a smile crossed her face as she recalled the precious memories she shared with her husband and how, after eight years of waiting, she conceived their son. How much light and love the child brought to them. She remembered his first steps and how disappointed she was that her husband was not present to witness them. As soon as she heard her husband's whistle, she knew he was nearby and would be coming up the dirt path. She swung open the door and helped little Samuel down the single stone step. Samuel's face lit into a big smile when he saw the toddler. "Come on son," he said as Stabat let go of the boy's tiny hands. After the child stumbled and fell, he stood back up and walked the few short steps to his father. As Samuel hoisted his son in the air, little Samuel waved his hands, something he always did when his father returned home from work.

Stabat's wonderful memories of her husband and son soon were swept away by the painful thoughts of losing her loved ones. She easily would have traded her own life to save either one of them. "Why?" she wondered. "Why did she have to lose them both?" All that she cherished had been taken from her. Stabat's heart was desolate, making her vengeance for the road bandit who had stolen her joy and purpose that much sweeter. An evil smile crept across her face, knowing that she was going to watch him die.

Stabat could not contain her anger. She picked up one of the wobbly wooden stools and flung it across the room. She watched as it floated through the air, as if in slow motion, before smashing against the wall, hitting the floor and breaking into pieces. "Oh Stabat, what have you done?" she thought as one of the stool legs whirled toward her, spinning on the dirt floor until it landed on the tip of her leather sandal. Her emotional outburst startled her, as she never had expressed hurt or anger that way before. And with that, she walked out the door.

She walked over to the garden. Even though she had scanned it many times, she hoped to find another fig or perhaps a handful of overlooked lentils. Her hunger pangs reminded her that she had picked everything in the garden that was edible. As she passed the garden fence, she drew a deep breath on her way to pay her respects to her beloved husband and son. After kneeling down besides their graves, she touched her fingers to her lips and then laid her fingers on each wooden grave marker. Standing up, she adjusted her shawl and did not look back as she walked down the path leading to the main road. Stabat's journey had begun.

~ • ~

Stabat walked steadily throughout the day, taking few breaks. Toward nightfall, her body grew weary and she knew she had to stop to rest. As she walked, she scoured the hillsides and fields for a cluster of bushes or trees to lie beneath. If she was to get any sleep and avoid being robbed, she knew she had to be out of sight, away from the road. Just before dusk, she spotted what appeared to be an old, abandoned hut among a grove of olive trees. Hungry and tired, she decided to stop and have a look. Inside she found a worn and tattered straw mattress on the dirt floor. The shabby shelter was better than sleeping on the ground, she thought, so she decided to stay for the night.

In the darkness, she slowly ate the bread and dried fish she had brought along. It would help her be strong for tomorrow. She wanted to eat one of the figs, and even brought one of them to her lips, but she thought better and put it back in the bucket.

In two days she would be in the city where, she was told, the thief would be punished. She would watch the man die who had brought her untold misery. She had every right to want to witness his suffering and death. After all, she was a penniless widow and, more importantly, a mother who had lost her only son.

She considered removing her shawl and using it as a makeshift pillow. Instead, she decided to retrieve a large stone that she had tripped over on her way to the hut. She laid the stone beneath a corner of the mattress as a headrest.

When she awoke the next morning, her stomach was aching for food, but she only allowed herself to eat one of the figs. But more than hunger was nagging Stabat. She also was tormented by a myriad of emotion swirling in her head as she recalled the tragic events that left her a widow and grieving mother.

Shortly after sunrise she resumed her journey. Before long, she arrived at a fork in the road, and trusting her memory, she took the route to the right. Because she had never been to the city, she hoped she remembered the directions imparted to her by a messenger who had visited her home a few weeks earlier. The young man had startled her. She was working outside in the garden when she heard an unfamiliar voice approach from behind. He meant no harm, he said. He only wanted to trouble her for a drink of water and to deliver a message to the woman of the house. When he confirmed that Stabat was the person to whom he was to deliver the message, he did just that. She listened intently as the messenger relayed details from Samuel's younger brother about the date and location where her husband's assailant would be put to death. News that the bandit had been captured was a gratifying revelation to Stabat who, for the first time since her husband and son's deaths, had a reason to live.

That night she couldn't sleep. She tossed and turned in her bed, wondering whether she could make the journey alone. By morning, she resolved that she was going to the city. She was going to watch his execution, she thought as she strode onward toward the city, still more than a day away.

As she walked, Stabat ruminated over the tragic events that led her on her justice-seeking journey. With each step in her dusty sandals, she thought about her last conversation with her husband. He had struggled with each dying breath as he told her about the fight he had with a road bandit who had stolen his money. A desperate, lawless man with a scar on his face had jumped him and fought mercilessly to steal the money that Samuel had stowed in his satchel. As Samuel fought, he begged the thief not to take the satchel. He tried to reason with the thief, explaining that he needed the money inside the bag to buy medicine for his son.

"Please, please," he begged as he fought. "My son, my only son is sick. He needs the medicine; the money is for his medicine!"

Samuel's frantic pleas were ignored. The assailant swung at Samuel one last time, and as he did, Samuel found himself falling back, falling down. He watched as the leather bag that held the coins slipped from his hand. As his head hit the ground, he could taste the blood running from his lip as the thief snatched the bag of coins and ran away.

Stabat mournfully remembered her last few hours with Samuel. She held his head in her lap, tending his wounds as the bucket of water in which she rinsed a rag turned red with blood. All the while, he kept mumbling about how a man with a scar below his left eye had jumped him, beaten him and stolen his money.

As she stopped for a drink of water, Stabat recalled how the messenger had told her that a well-known thief with a scar on his face was going to be executed in the city for his crimes. The gratifying thought motivated her to keep walking.

She had not been on the road long when she was startled by what appeared to be a man lying on the side of the road. As she got closer, she realized that she could see the outline of more than one human figure. She was unsure what to do. She did not have time to hide or wait until they left. Fretfully, she kept walking toward them. Soon she discovered three men sprawled on the ground. One lay completely on the road, one a few feet off the road under a tree and the other was curled up near a bush with one leg on the road. They all were asleep. From the empty jugs strewn on the ground, she concluded that they were drunk and had passed out from overindulgence. Even though she doubted that they would awaken anytime soon, she scurried past them, her eyes darting at each man as she stayed on the other side of the road. She walked quietly and quickly, and the only noises she heard were their loud snores.

Much to her surprise, Stabat discovered a large cloth sack tied to the lower limb of a tree only a few yards from the sleeping men. She suspected the sack contained food and had been tied to the limb to prevent animals from getting inside. The men would be looking for it when they woke up. She figured they would blame each other as she took the sack and tried to stuff it into her small bucket. When it failed to fit, she emptied the contents onto the ground and packed four pieces of dried fish, a cluster of dates and half-dozen figs in the bucket. She quickly tore a piece from a loaf of bread and stuffed it into her mouth while she tucked the rest of the loaf into the scarf around her waist. When she discarded the cloth bag under the tree, she found three more empty jugs. She considered taking one of them with her should she find water, but she decided against it. "Fools," she thought as she bid farewell to the sleeping sots and hurried down the road. "A herd of camels could not wake them."

Once she was out of sight, Stabat found a shade tree and sat down beneath it. She pulled a piece of fish out of the bucket and savored every bite along with a small portion of the bread. She finished off her meal with two delicious dates. With her stomach full and renewed vigor, she was able to walk much faster. Before she knew it, the sun was setting and she began her search for a place to bed down. She soon found a thicket of bushes near a dry riverbed. Exhausted from the long walk, she lay down and immediately fell asleep. She slept soundly through most of the night, awakened only once by the howls of hunting jackals.

In the morning, she devoured two of the figs and ate the last of the bread. Fed and refreshed, she returned to the road to finish the last leg of her journey. As she walked, her thoughts turned to the forthcoming execution of the road bandit. He deserved his fate, she kept repeating to herself. For Stabat, watching the criminal die seemed the only way to alleviate her pain. She wanted him to suffer a slow, dreadful death, a death more agonizing than her husband and son had experienced. She would delight in his torment. Justice would be the thread to mend her broken heart.

Mile after mile Stabat walked with determination. Past the olive groves and barley fields she traveled, until she could see the city's stone walls in the distance.

~ • ~

The closer Stabat got to the city, the more people she passed on the road. As she walked, she overheard conversations among the passersby. Three criminals were to be put to death. They were to be crucified on a hill outside the city.

As she approached the walls of the city, the crowds grew thicker and Stabat became more nervous. The time for justice was at hand, yet now that she was in its midst, she was uncertain that she wanted to witness an execution. Amid the noise and congestion, she could see a mass of people gathering at the base of a hill in the distance. Atop the hill, she could see the silhouettes of three crosses standing stark against the azure sky. Her heart almost skipped a beat at the sight of the spectacle. She had arrived. She finally was going to get the restitution she deserved for enduring months of tearful, sleepless nights, and empty, mournful days filled with pain and misery.

As Stabat maneuvered through the crowd, it became apparent that some of the spectators had been camped at the execution site for several days. Slowly she inched through the assembly of people, making her way up the hill to get closer to the crosses. After a final push through the mass of curious onlookers, the moment she had been waiting for arrived. She could see the man with the scar across his left cheek. His sullen grimace told of his torment.

She stood speechless, gazing upon the thief who had stolen so much from her. He hung on the wooden cross to the left. While the cross in the middle stood taller than the ones on either side, Stabat remained fixated on the one on the left. Even though she was not as close to the thief as she wanted to be, she thought he might see her. "Maybe he will see me smile," she thought. "There will be no tears today! Maybe he will wonder, 'Who is this woman smiling at me?' And maybe, just maybe, he will know who I am. Maybe he will know that the two people most important in my life are dead because of him."

Being small in stature, Stabat managed to squeeze into the front row of the dense crowd, though Roman soldiers posted around the crosses prevented her from advancing any farther.

When someone near her shouted "Jesus," Stabat momentarily stopped glaring at the thief. She did not know who this Jesus was or what crimes he had committed, though she was certain if he hung next to the bandit on his right, he must have committed a horrible crime and deserved to die. After all, since he was nailed to the taller cross in the middle, he must be the most wretched of the three criminals. "It serves you right," she thought. But as soon as her thought ended, a cold shudder ran through her body and she almost collapsed to the ground. She did not fall, however. She stood strong in her righteousness.

As the day wore on, Stabat wandered through the crowd, listening to the chatter and stories about Jesus. Some claimed he was innocent.

Others said he deserved to die. The provincial governor Pontius Pilate reportedly had found no fault with Jesus, so why did so many others? Why had Pilate washed his hands of the matter?

Stabat strained her neck to look around. Once again, she slowly pushed through the crowd toward the top of the hill. She managed to get a little closer to the three crucified men. But instead of staring at the thief on the left, a woman at the base of the middle cross caught her attention. Tears streamed from the woman's eyes and she was consumed by grief. It seemed as if all the pain that Stabat had experienced could be seen on the woman's face. A friend stood next to the woman, stroking her long hair, trying to console her and absorbing her tears with an already damp cloth. She discovered that the grieving woman's name was Mary and that it was her son, Jesus, hanging on the middle cross.

Some in the crowd said Jesus was a prophet. Others called him a heretic. His followers referred to him as the son of God and claimed he had been sent from heaven. Stabat did not understand the concept of heaven. Instead, she stood staring at Mary.

Observing Mary's pain reminded her of her own. She remembered how she had cradled little Samuel in her arms, frantically trying to comfort him. With each passing hour, it seemed as if his painful cries grew louder. The time spent waiting for her husband to return with the boy's medicine was heart wrenching. "What had happened to him?" she wondered. Time and again that question kept churning in her mind. She considered going to one of the nearby villages to look for her husband, but she didn't know exactly where he had gone. Furthermore, she knew she could not carry sick little Samuel very far and she would not risk leaving him alone. She tried bathing the boy in cool water, but nothing seemed to calm him. His little body was burning with fever. As his condition worsened, he refused to eat and eventually he only drank small sips of water, not enough to keep him alive.

Gradually, the cries of her dying child turned to whimpers. She watched helplessly as her son's breathing grew slow and shallow, and eventually stopped. When little Samuel died in her arms, oh how she cried. She did not want to let him go, so she held him close until his feverish body grew cold. She kissed his face, his little arms and begged him to come back to life. She could not recall how long she sat with him in her lap. All she remembers is her unbearable anguish.

Alone, Stabat dug a grave and buried her son. That night she slept on his grave. It was too painful to leave him. When she awoke the next morning and was making her way to the house, she discovered her husband lying near the garden gate. He was bloodied, bruised and his face so badly beaten that it was almost unrecognizable. She rushed to grab a bucket of water and a cloth to wipe the dried blood from his face. She struggled to understand the faint words he uttered to her before he died. He told her that a man had beaten and robbed him before he could buy little Samuel's medicine. As he lay half-conscious and bleeding on the roadside, a kind passerby stopped to give him a drink of water and bandage his wounds. Somehow during the night he found the wherewithal to stagger home. Before the day was done, Stabat was digging another grave next to her son's.

~ • ~

The shouts of Roman soldiers barking commands to the crowd shook Stabat from her subconscious. "How much time had passed?" she wondered. She wasn't certain.

As she blended into the clamorous crowd, she heard more stories about Jesus, his blessings and many wonders. Again, some claimed that he was the son of God, sent to bring hope and peace to all those who would listen to and embrace his teachings. They spoke of heaven as a place of eternal peace, but Stabat could not envision such a place. Others spoke about how Jesus had preached about forgiveness of sin. One man claimed to have seen Jesus heal a blind beggar and cure people of their diseases. But others argued he was a false prophet or heretic.

Watching the thief suffer on the cross and hearing others speak joyfully of his impending death did not bring Stabat the relief she had expected. Instead, a much deeper ache took its place. She missed her husband and son dearly. Thoughts of them brought back memories of that fateful morning. She sensed something was wrong. Her baby's curdling cry was different than his usual cry of hunger. His eyes were watery and his lively smile was gone. By evening, he refused to eat and his little body was clammy and burning with fever. The next morning her husband tucked a few coins they had saved into his satchel and set off for a nearby village to buy medicine for their sick son. But Samuel never made it to the village.

Suddenly, Stabat's recollections were interrupted as the Roman soldiers mocked Jesus and provoked an exchange between the condemned men. The crowd was murmuring and hushing, eager to overhear the conversation. Some hoped Jesus' words would allow them to condemn him for the false prophet they thought he was. And then, as the crowd grew quiet, Stabat heard the thief—a murderer as far as she was concerned—speak.

"We deserve to die for our crimes, but this man hasn't done anything wrong." Then the thief turned to Jesus and said, "Lord, remember me when you come into your kingdom."

Stabat was beside herself. Had she heard his words correctly? Had the thief admitted to his crimes? Did he realize that not only had he beaten her husband and stolen the coins meant to buy her son's medicine, but that his misdeeds had resulted in the deaths of both her husband and her son? Did he know what he had taken from her? She wanted to shake her fist at him. "You stole my son and my husband. They are dead, gone from my life forever because of you," she thought. The pain welled up in her heart and sorrow once again overtook her. Stricken with grief, she could not move or speak.

Was he accepting his responsibility? Was he admitting to all of his crimes and wrongdoing? "Good!" she thought.

She tried to move closer to the thief. "Tell him! Tell that Jesus what you took from me!" Stabat screamed.

Stabat's futile pleas were overwhelmed by the commotion as throngs of people pressed forward toward the crosses. "Move back, move back," the soldiers shouted as they repelled the riotous and unruly mob with their shields, swords and spears.

Angry people in the crowd chanted: "Die! Die!" and "You deserve what you are getting."

The thief was weakening. His head slumped to the side as he struggled to keep his eyes on Jesus. Then Jesus spoke to the thief in a strong voice that echoed so loudly that men shuddered. "Truly, I say to you, today you will be with me in paradise."

Stabat could not believe what she had heard. She could not bear the mercy of Jesus' words and she dropped to her knees. How could this lawless criminal be forgiven? Was this the peace, salvation and heaven that so many people in the crowd had spoken about? She couldn't breathe. The pain and heartbreak of losing her husband and child were as fresh as the day they had died. She couldn't bear the clash of her conflicting emotions. If Jesus had so much power, then why didn't he punish the thief?

"Ask me, Jesus. Ask me, what he took from me," she pleaded. "How many other horrific crimes has he committed? It isn't fair."

"And how could this Jesus pardon sin?" she thought. "How could he promise a sinner paradise?"

As anger surged inside, Stabat felt as if she were spinning around. Her vision began to blur. Was she going to pass out? In the heat of the crowd, she could feel that something was happening that she could not control. She looked down at her hand. A sharp chunk of wood was stuck in it. She recognized the wood from the stool she had flung across the room. She was squeezing the piece of wood so tightly that blood was dripping from her palm. She did not know how the wood got there, but she could not let it go. Though it was a warm day, the air suddenly felt cold to Stabat. Amid the noisy crowd, silence seemed to envelop her. People were all around but no one was offering to help her. She tried to speak but she couldn't, and as a chill ran through her body, she fell to the ground. Blood was streaming down her arm onto her tunic as she gripped the piece of wood in her hand. She couldn't let it go and then she lost consciousness.

Stabat didn't know how much time had passed while she was unconscious, yet she knew someone was close to her, speaking to her. His voice was calm and reassuring, and his hand was on her forehead. As she slowly opened her eyes, she could see the feet of many people around her, but she could not hear their voices. And to them, it was as if she didn't exist. She turned her head toward the person who was speaking to her. It was Jesus! The man who had been nailed to the center cross was kneeling by her side, holding her hand and looking lovingly into her eyes. He wasn't covered in blood, and his hands showed no signs of nail marks.

"How was this possible?" she wondered. "How could it be? How could he have gotten down off the cross?" She was confused.

As Jesus put his hand on her chest, she felt something happening inside of her. She could feel the pain of her losses dissipating. Though she was confounded, she was not afraid. She cried out: "My child, my child is gone! My husband, my husband; he is gone, too." Jesus kept his hand on her chest, absorbing all of her anger, pain and sorrow and exchanging them for forgiveness and peace.

"I know. I know," he said, his eyes conveying a hope that she had not experienced since her husband and son's deaths.

Stabat attempted to speak, but she could not. She closed her eyes and fell asleep.

When she regained consciousness for the second time, she found that her palm had stopped bleeding and that her hand was wrapped in a cloth. She soon recognized that the fabric was a piece of the swaddling cloth that she had wrapped her son in when he was born. She wasn't certain what had happened. She felt disoriented. Had she fallen asleep? Had she fainted? The man on the cross that the crowd called Jesus, was it really him who had kneeled beside her? Many people remained around her, but it was as if she were invisible to them. She closed her eyes again.

When she awoke for the third time, she was leaning against an olive tree. She looked down at her hand. The swaddling cloth was gone. She found no piece of wood in her palm, no wound or blood. It did not hurt. What had happened?

"Was it real? Had Jesus spoken to her and held her hand?" she asked. "It was real, wasn't it?"

Stabat knew it was real because her heart was lighter. The hatred she had harbored was gone and a serenity she never had experienced had taken its place. She stood up and was going to make her way through the crowd. She had to get to Jesus. Though he was bloody and bruised, it was he who had knelt beside her and comforted her. It was he who had laid his hand on her chest and relieved her burdened and grieving heart.

She began singing, "Jesus, Jesus." Over and over she sang, "Jesus, Jesus."

Tragically, before she could reach him, he took his last breath. Stabat was distressed. "No," she thought. "This could not happen." She had not thanked him for what he had done for her. Tears of regret filled her eyes. She fell to her knees, wailing and weeping.

"Oh no, Jesus! Oh no, Jesus," she cried. "I did not want you to die."

Stabat stayed on the hillside beneath the crosses until all three men were declared dead. She stayed even as the crowd began to disperse. As the crowd thinned, she was able to get a closer look at Mary. Jesus' mother was on her knees, slumped over, rocking her body slightly. Two women stood close to her, occasionally offering her sips of water and pieces of bread. They patted her forehead with a cloth and pulled back strands of hair that had fallen over her face.

Before the bodies and crosses were taken down, most of the crowd was gone. Dusk turned to night, but Stabat refused to leave. She lay on the hard ground and slept on and off until dawn. She stirred when she heard voices of the soldiers, who were dismantling and removing the crosses. Even after the soldiers left, she lingered. She did not want to leave the spot where Jesus had visited her. And where was she to go? She had not planned to return to her home, but now it seemed that her home held precious memories rather than painful losses. Hesitantly, she began her journey home. For the first time in many months, Stabat felt a sense of relief and she shed tears of joy.

Stabat was almost home when she saw a man approaching her on the road. She was not frightened and, as she got closer, she realized it was him, it was Jesus. She ran to him. "I saw you die! I saw you die!" she cried. "But you are here. How are you here?"

Jesus smiled, held out his hands and she saw the scars. She took his hands and held them to her cheek. Together, they stood on the road in silence. She wondered how much time had passed: a minute, an hour or maybe a lifetime? However long, within a blink of an eye, Stabat was standing alone on the road. But for the first time since she had lost her husband and son, she did not feel alone.

The evening sun was setting as Stabat walked up the path to her home. When she opened the door, enough light remained to see inside. She managed to start a fire in the hearth. Out of habit, she reached for the lamp and lit it. She was perplexed. She was certain she had used the last of the oil before she left. The lamp lit up the room and Stabat stood at the kitchen table in astonishment. Though she was puzzled at first, a large smile swept across her face when she noticed the stool, the one that she had thrown across the room, the one she had watched smash into pieces was sitting in the middle of the room restored, just like her heart.

STABAT MATER

The name Stabat is taken from "Stabat Mater," a 13th-century hymn, which depicts the suffering of Jesus Christ's mother. In Latin, *stabat mater dolorosa*, the first line in the hymn, translates to "the sorrowful mother was standing."

ABOUT THE AUTHOR

Roschelle Ridenhour also is the author of "The Cottage Porch Stories," published by Rock Dreams Press. She has written various Bible studies, songs and short stories.

www.ingramcontent.com/pod-product-compliance
Lightning Source LLC
Chambersburg PA
CBHW021147020426
42331CB00005B/941